FOREWORD

This book is a celebration of life on farms in Ireland, through the eyes and words of children. They tell us that farms are great places to live and grow up on. They also tell us how fragile life on the farm can be for children and adults alike, when chances are taken and safety is compromised. Their words and pictures are a reminder to all those making their livelihood on farms of how preventable accidents are, and the truth about the chances that get taken every day of the week on farms in Ireland. It might be a near miss today. Tomorrow it could be a serious injury or fatality. On average, 21 people die in farm-related accidents each year. Many more are seriously injured. Farms remain the only workplace in Ireland where children still continue to die. Those in farming owe it to themselves and their families to prevent these tragedies, which are often compounded by happening in what is both home and workplace. A huge change in mind-set is needed to move away from taking unnecessary risks, if we are to change the outlook for a new generation.

The stories and images in the book were written and produced by children aged between five and twelve, from all over Ireland who answered the call to enter a HSA art/story-writing competition. From more than 9,500 entries, 86 children won and were given the opportunity to work with artists, writers and each other to produce this book. Copies will be available in every school and library in the country.

Thank you to our partners in Kilkenny Education Centre and the other 20 full-time Education Centres for helping us get the farm safety message into every primary school. A huge thanks also to Kids' Own Publishing Partnership whose artists and writers let the voices of children be heard so clearly and beautifully in this book. Let us now heed those voices and act upon them to make work-related deaths on farms a thing of the past.

Martin O' Halloran, CEO, Health and Safety Authority

1

MIDLANDS

ATHLONE EDUCATION CENTRE

Anna Galvin, Senior Infants
Mount Talbot NS, Co. Roscommon

Roísín Walsh, 1st Class
St Feichin's NS, Castlepollard, Co. Westmeath

Eva Isdell, 3rd Class
St Cremin's NS, Multyfarnham, Co. Westmeath

Sophia Dorgan, 5th Class
Coralstown NS, Mullingar, Co. Westmeath

CLARE EDUCATION CENTRE

Aisling Heapes, Senior Infants
Querrin NS, Kilkee, Co. Clare

Alanna Hayes, 2nd Class
Rineen NS, Miltown Malbay, Co. Clare

Bláthnaid Marsh, 4th Class
St Enda's NS, Lisdoonvarna, Co. Clare

Stephen Kennedy, 5th Class
Bodyke NS, Bodyke, Co. Clare

LAOIS EDUCATION CENTRE

Heidi Whitten, Senior Infants
Maryboro NS, Portlaoise, Co. Laois

Adam Schuch, 1st Class
Paddock NS, Paddock, Mountrath, Co. Laois

Aisling Carroll, 4th Class
Wolfhill NS, Athy, Co. Kildare

Éire Lawless, 5th Class
Rosenallis NS, Co. Laois

GALWAY EDUCATION CENTRE

Sadhbh Ní Fhlaithearta, 3rd Class
Scoil Einne, An Spideal, Co. Galway

Saoirse Melia, Senior Infants
Lavally NS, Lavally, Tuam, Co. Galway

Sarah Noone, 6th Class
Scoil Mhuire Naofa, Menlough, Co. Galway

Donal Reilly, 2nd Class
Ballymana NS, Craughwell, Co. Galway

NORTH WEST

SLIGO EDUCATION CENTRE

Adam McMahon Coleman, 1st Class
St Joseph's NS, Culleens, Co. Sligo

Christopher Twydell, 5th Class
St Mary's NS, Kilrusheighter, Templeboy, Co. Sligo

Shannagh Gallagher, Senior Infants
St Teresa's NS, Ballintogher, Co. Sligo

Nicole Murphy, 4th Class
Scoil Críost, Enniscrone, Co. Sligo

CARRICK-ON-SHANNON EDUCATION CENTRE

Rachel Durr, 4th Class
St. Mary's NS, Ballinagare, Co. Roscommon

Eva Greene, 2nd Class
Roxboro NS, Derrane, Co. Roscommon

Annabelle Frankham, Junior Infants
Hunt NS, Mohill, Co. Leitrim

Daniel Moorhead, 5th Class
St John's NS, Edgeworthstown, Co. Longford

DONEGAL EDUCATION CENTRE

Adam McCracken, 3rd Class
Castletown NS, St Johnston, Co. Donegal

Hannah Rose Deane, Senior Infants
Killaghtee NS, Co. Donegal

Jason Arthur, 5th Class
Castletown NS, St Johnston, Co. Donegal

Jasmine Glackin, 2nd Class
Scoil Mhuire, Malin Head, Co. Donegal

MAYO EDUCATION CENTRE

Alice Curran, 1st Class
St Brigid's NS, Tooreen, Ballyhaunis, Co. Mayo

Emma McManamon, 3rd Class
Drumgallagh NS, Ballycroy, Westport, Co. Mayo

Emma O'Brien, Junior Infants
Logboy NS, Bekan, Claremorris, Co. Mayo

Meabh Byron, 6th Class
Scoil Mhuire, Glencorrib, Shrule, Co. Mayo

NORTH EAST

NAVAN EDUCATION CENTRE

Ava Mullan, Junior Infants
Rathmore NS, Athboy, Co. Meath

Fionn Mullan, Senior Infants
Rathmore NS, Athboy, Co. Meath

Shauna Murphy, 2nd Class
Scoil Mhuire, Carlanstown, Co. Meath

Abby Eogan, 4th Class
Nobber NS, Nobber, Co. Meath

Gavin Nolan Hackett, 5th Class
St Ultan's School, Navan, Co. Meath

DRUMCONDRA EDUCATION CENTRE

Meadhbh Brennan, 4th Class
St Columba's NS, Navan, Co. Meath

Georgiana Ciornei, 4th Class
St Columba's NS, Navan, Co. Meath

Emma Doyle, 4th Class
St Mary's NS, Garristown, Co. Dublin

Emily Mangan, 4th Class
St Mary's NS, Garristown, Co. Dublin

MONAGHAN EDUCATION CENTRE

Amy Rhatigan, Senior Infants
St. Mary's NS, Threemilehouse, Co. Monaghan

Brady Maguire, 3rd Class
St Patrick's NS, Lisboduff, Cootehill, Co. Cavan

Conor McEnaney, 2nd Class
Scoil Phadraig, Corduff, Co. Monaghan

Patrick Smith, 6th Class
Killyconnan NS, Co. Cavan

THANK

EAST

DUBLIN WEST EDUCATION CENTRE

Erica Mae Bacani, 1st Class
St Ciaran's NS, Clonsilla, Dublin 15

Kerri McCann, 6th Class
St Ciaran's NS, Clonsilla, Dublin 15

Ruby Nixon, Junior Infants
St Andrew's NS, Lucan, Co. Kildare

Nathan White, 3rd Class
St Andrew's NS, Lucan, Co. Kildare

BLACKROCK EDUCATION CENTRE

Faye Megarity, 2nd Class
Moneystown NS, Co. Wicklow

Eleanor Stephens, 3rd Class,
St Patrick's NS, Curtlestown, Co. Wicklow

Dean Harris, 5th Class
Oliver Plunkett School, Monkstown, Co. Dublin

William Smith, Junior Infants
Nun's Cross NS, Ashford, Co. Wicklow

KILDARE EDUCATION CENTRE

Ciana Dunne, 4th Class
Allen NS, Allen, Co. Kildare

Lily Raben, 2nd Class
Hewetson NS, Millicent, Co. Kildare

Milena Modesto, 6th Class
Piper's Hill CNS, Naas, Co. Kildare

Toby McMorland, Senior Infants
St Joseph's BNS, Kilcock, Co. Kildare

SOUTH WEST

THE EDUCATION CENTRE TRALEE

Lily Ashe, Senior Infants
Scoil Breac Chluain, Annascaul, Co. Kerry

Cathal McElligott, 2nd Class
Loughfounder NS, Co. Kerry

Tadhg Griffin, 4th Class
Glenderry NS, Ballyheigue, Co. Kerry

Kevin O'Connor, 6th Class
Meenkilly NS, Abbeyfeale, Co. Limerick

LIMERICK EDUCATION CENTRE

Benjamin O'Dwyer, 6th Class
Doon CBS, Doon, Co. Limerick

Ethan O'Connell, 4th Class
Ardpatrick NS, Ardpatrick, Co. Limerick

John Ryan, 2nd Class
Templederry NS, Nenagh, Co. Tipperary

Corie Lynch, Senior Infants
Feenagh NS, Killmallock, Co. Limerick

CORK EDUCATION SUPPORT CENTRE

Samantha Streit, Senior Infants
Rylane NS, Rylane, Co. Cork

Danny Fitzgerald, 2nd Class
Inch NS, Killeagh, Co. Cork

Pádraic O'Sullivan, 4th Class
Rylane NS, Rylane, Co. Cork

Jessica Griffin, 5th Class
St. Killian's NS, Bishopstown, Co. Cork

WEST CORK EDUCATION CENTRE

Eimear McCarthy, Senior Infants
Scoil Eoin, Innishannon, Co. Cork

Gráinne McCarthy, 2nd Class
Derrinacahara NS, Dunmanway, Co. Cork

Róisín Ní Riordáin, 4th Class
Scoil Chúil Aodha Bárr d Ínse, Co. Cork

Olivia Shortall, 6th Class
St Mary's NS, Enniskeane, Co. Cork

SOUTH EAST

KILKENNY EDUCATION CENTRE

Holly Hughes, 2nd Class
Glenmore NS, Co. Kilkenny

Jack Mullally, 4th Class
Shanbogh NS, Co. Kilkenny

Sophie Ryan, 6th Class
Ballinure NS, Co. Tipperary

Mante Sladkeviciúte, Infants
Newtown Dunleckney NS, Co. Carlow

Niamh Ryan, 6th Class
Scoil Íosagáin, Thurles, Co. Tipperary

WATERFORD TEACHERS CENTRE

Oscar Brunnock, 1st Class
Rathgormack NS, Rathgormack, Co. Waterford

Béibhínn Delaney, Senior Infants
Seafield NS, Seafield, Co. Waterford

Caoimhe Perdue, 6th Class
St John the Baptist GNS, Cashel, Co. Tipperary

Seán Hayes, 3rd Class
Portlaw NS, Portlaw, Co. Waterford

WEXFORD EDUCATION CENTRE

Chafia Flynn, Senior Infants
Our Lady of Lourdes NS, Bunclody, Co. Wexford

Emma Ryan, 4th Class
Ballon NS, Ballon, Co. Carlow

Kieran Condren, 5th Class
St Joseph's NS, Templerainey, Co.Wicklow

Tara McDonald, 2nd Class
St Brigid's NS, Crossbridge, Co. Wicklow

YOU!

MIDLANDS

The things I like most about being on the farm... I like listening to the sound of the **BEES**, because there's long grass and flowers all around. When you're there you have to be careful that you don't step into a bit of mud, because once I did and I got my foot stuck in it. I got my foot out but I didn't get the shoe out. The worst thing about living on the farm is the smell of slurry or the fertilizer. The fertilizer smells bad! My uncle got rid of the horns on the bull – for safety. But the FEMALE COWS CAN BE MORE ANGRY THAN THE MALES.

We feed the cows hay and silage and seeds and nuts and they graze a lot at the field. My uncle has this machine that goes on the back of the tractor and you put the timber into it and it drops and it chops it up. If you have your finger there and you leave it down you could lose one. We were climbing on the hay bales and my friend stepped down a hole right between them and HE COULDN'T GET OUT so we had to gently tip them over so he could crawl out.

Stephen Kennedy, 5th Class, Co. Clare

My granddad has a farm but the only animals he has are **PHEASANTS**. He grows barley. I've seen it in the field. I think they're growing fruit trees as well. My cousins live up there next to my granny so we walk up to their house to see them. We play on the farm but we don't go near any of the machinery. My granddad would say 'don't be climbing on it, cause you could fall off and hurt yourself.'

They have a big shed and it has loads of wood in it and beside that there's loads of old machinery and sometimes my little brother climbs up on it and we have to tell him to come down because he might fall off. At my uncle's house he has swings and slides so we're allowed to go on them.

Eva Isdell, 3rd Class, Co. Westmeath

I was wearing red and my mammy saw the **BULL** and she hid me behind her back but luckily the bull didn't see me. Sometimes they can have horns but this one didn't have horns. Sometimes cows can have horns as well.
Granddad has a farm. IF I EVER GO DOWN IN THE FIELDS I GO WITH MY DADDY. He sometimes helps out my granddad. Sometimes I stay in the house and sometimes I help them. I went down the fields with them. I collected the hen's eggs, just me and my brother and my granddad. But we don't do it anymore.

4

Saoirse Melia, Senior Infants, Co. Galway

One time my mum was out on the **HORSE** and the horse put its head down to graze and my mum just slid down its head. We have chickens and bees so we can get a bit of money from the eggs and the honey. And we had a cockerel one time and his name was Homer because he was always eating the chicken feed. All the cockerels have these little knife things on their legs and twice I went in to get the eggs and he got me on the ankles so we ate him. I have to get the eggs and clean the chicken house and with the bees I have to help daddy to lift the frames and put the honey in the jars and sell it. You have to wear a bee suit and put a veil on your face in case the bees try stinging you and the stinger can't get you.

MY DAD GOT STUNG BY A BEE ON THE EYE AND IT SWELLED UP AND HIS EYE GOT SMALLER AND SMALLER AND SMALLER.

My friend has a wild bull and it's really dangerous because it's so hairy you can't see its horns.

Adam Schuch, 1st Class, Co. Laois

My granddad, when he was on his farm, he was doing something with the **HOOF** of the cow and the cow didn't like it, so he kicked my granddad on the knee. And my granddad fell down, but he didn't have a phone on him.

And my grandma was waiting for him at home. She had the dinner ready and she was waiting on him to come in and after two hours she went looking for him, and she found him lying on the ground.

FARMERS OFTEN DO THINGS ON THEIR OWN. IF YOU HAVE YOUR MOBILE YOU CAN PHONE OR TEXT.

Aisling Carroll, 4th Class, Co. Kildare

Don't go in the field with lots of **CATTLE** in it, because if you open the gate, they'll run out. Horses could kick you and bulls could chase after you. Donkeys are really strong and they could knock down a fence. My cat Alice eats wasps and bees and flies and ladybirds and insects and things like that. My teacher's uncle got his leg tore off by a PTO shaft. You shouldn't go in front of a tractor.

BE CAREFUL OF MACHINERY. IT COULD KILL YOU OR SQUASH YOU OR TEAR YOUR LEG OFF OR POKE YOUR EYE OUT.

Róisin Walsh, 1st Class, Co. Westmeath

My granny has a farm and daddy and Noel and Seán look after the **COWS** and sheep. Once I helped them close the gate. I'm allowed to go on the farm only if I ask.

I DON'T PLAY IN THE HAY BALES. Sometimes my cousin Niall jumps on them. There's no more hay left. We're going to cut a field beside my house so we can make bales out of it. They cut it and then they turn it round and then they wrap it up in some plastic that's black. They have tractors and there's this thing on the back and some kind of thing that turns it into a bale and it goes onto another machine and it wraps it all into the plastic.

Anna Galvin, Senior Infants, Co. Roscommon

I have six **DOGS** and we were at the lane and we passed the farm and then one of my dogs – Shelby – she nearly ran in. We saw some cows in the field and some bulls. My mam grabbed her and just put her on the lead. She could have got chased by a cow or a bull and one of us might have had to go in after her and we could have got hurt. Make sure you always have the dogs on the lead when you pass anything or if they go into the field try and call them back without going in.

Sophia Dorgan, 5th Class, Co. Westmeath

I have a friend who lives on a farm. It's a dairy farm. I've never been on it. I've been on my granddad's farm, but he's not really a farmer anymore, he just looks after animals – **HORSES** and donkeys. My sister goes out to pet them but you have to be careful of them.

Sarah Noone, 6th Class, Co. Galway

My brother works on the farm with my dad. He's six. I don't know what he does. He says it's fun. My dad keeps an eye on him. He usually does it on a Saturday while I'm at dancing. Sometimes they go to the **BOG** and they cut the turf. They do different things. If I ask my dad I would be allowed to go to the farm but usually I stay at home.

Alanna Hayes, 2nd Class, Co. Clare

6

My friends in Kilkenny have a **STUD FARM.** It's smelly. We made a swing out of a wheel. They told me not to go near their greyhounds because one of them can bite. They have nine horses. Sometimes I feel safe around the horses. But they told us not to go behind them, because they won't be able to see you and then they'll just kick.

YOU ALWAYS HAVE TO GO IN FRONT OF THEM TO SEE WHAT YOU'RE DOING.

Sadhbh Ní Fhlaithearta, 3rd Class, Co. Galway

I live near a farm. They have fields and **COWS**. We just walk on the road beside it. I've been to my friend's farm. We were inside a shed and we went in this old shack.

Once when me and my brother were playing and kicking the ball around, there was a bull in the field opposite us and Oisín was wearing a red t-shirt and it started to charge and Oisín my brother started to get really scared and he came back up with a blue t-shirt.

Bláithnaid Marsh, 4th Class, Co. Clare

My cousin - one of the **HORSES** stood on her and she had two hook bruises on her belly. They shot the horse after that because it went all wild and started running all over the place.

THEY HAVE TWO BILLY GOATS AS WELL. ONE OF THEM HAD BIG MASSIVE HORNS AND HE CHARGED AT MY UNCLE'S WIFE AND SHE HURT HER LEG.

Éire Lawless, 5th Class, Co. Laois

We have a **BEEF FARM** in Co. Donegal. We have lots of cows and we have sheep too. CUTTING SILAGE. YOU HAVE TO BE CAREFUL BECAUSE IT'S A BUSY TIME. If you were buck raking silage you could tip off the pit. The buck rake has spikes. It's a square thing and there's two spikes out the side and one below and there's another thing then that pushes the silage off whenever you get back to the silage pit. We cut barley too, and it's dangerous too, because if you were walking across the fields while they were cutting with the combine you could get badly cut.

I keep listening for tractors to stay safe. If you see a cattle shed you'll know there's a slurry pit nearby. First you have to use a slurry mixer that mixes up the slurry and you have to step onto the machine and you could slip on the machine and fall into it then. If you had the arm up on the teleporter you could tip up. And DON'T STAND UNDER THE LOADER. If you didn't see it coming down, it could kill you.

The old tractors wouldn't be the easy ones, but the new tractors would be easy. The old ones have gears and levers. With the new one, you only have to press buttons with the gears. THERE IS A SEATBELT ON THE DRIVER'S SEAT BUT THERE'S NOT ONE ON THE PASSENGER SEAT. I SUPPOSE THERE SHOULD BE.

Adam McCracken, 3rd Class, Co. Donegal

Some of my friends live on farms. The farm is not a playground.

Emma O'Brien, Junior Infants, Co. Mayo

My dad's farm is just behind his uncle's house. It's **MESSY** and smelly. Once my dad brought my two younger brothers up to the shed and it was really windy. He went inside to give an injection to the cow and he told them to wait outside and the gate was open and the wind blew the gate and it hit my brother on the head and the blood was spurting everywhere. DON'T STAND TOO CLOSE TO THE GATE.

Rachel Durr, 4th Class, Co. Roscommon

My granddad has a farm. There were little **SILAGE PITS** and he had a little bottle of something but I don't know what it was and he had to pour it on the silage every day to keep it fresh. We weren't allowed to touch it. He said if you touched it, you might die. I like my granddad to put the fresh stuff on the silage because the smell of it goes away.

Shannagh Gallagher, Senior Infants, Co. Sligo

I fed **CALVES** and pet lambs. I fed them at my friend's house. I saw a shed, a tractor, sheep and cows. I go over to the house a good bit but I don't go onto the farm often. We don't go to the farm to play. CHILDREN NEED TO BE SUPERVISED AT ALL TIMES. If you don't close the gates a calf could get out too.

Meabh Byron, 6th Class, Co. Mayo

My granddad has a farm, he has cows and **SHEEP**. Sometimes I go there, usually on a Tuesday. I'm only allowed to go around the farm if I'm with my Granddad. We go in the shed to see the new borns. We have to be careful of Percy the bull. The cows are in a separate shed and they have their own cage. He has a tractor and some trailers for the cows. Last Saturday, my cousins came up and we had to put the sheep into the trailer. It's not too difficult to chase them out. We halted them back from the road because the cars were coming.

Jasmine Glackin, 2nd Class, Co. Donegal

I feed some of the cattle when I come home from school. I got chased by a **BULL** once. I fell in the field and it started running towards me. Never have raggy trousers, because the PTO could catch on them and it could take your leg off. It could kill you because it's going so fast. My dad tells me to keep away from them.

WE WERE MOVING A BATH FOR THE CATTLE UNDER A FENCE AND IT FELL ON MY DAD AND HE WAS UNDER IT AND IT BROKE HIS LEG JUST AT THE WAIST.

We wear steel toecap boots, so that if anything falls on your toe you can't get hurt. I like the smells on the farm especially silage just after it's been cut. I even like the dung smells!

Daniel Moorhead, 5th Class, Co. Longford

We have weedkiller and **BVD** and my dad has all these medicines for injecting the cows and branding paint. It has a horrible smell. In his slatted shed there's all these cabinets and shelves. If I wanted to go opening the presses I wouldn't be able to because it's locked. The bottles always have tight lids and labels. YOU NEED GOGGLES WHEN YOU'RE SPRAYING AND WHEN YOU'RE WITH THE STRIMMER. And when you're cleaning out the slatted shed you need to wear protective glasses because the gas is very strong.

My uncle, when he was only six, he saw this thing spinning at the back of the tractor and it was parked at the back of the yard. He went towards it because he thought it looked interesting. It was spinning round really fast. He put his finger out and the top of his finger came off and he had to go to the hospital to get a bit of skin from his back put onto his finger.

Eva Greene, 2nd Class, Co. Roscommon

I live on a **HORSE** farm. All my family ride horses. You ride and you clean out stables. If you're ever standing behind a horse he could kick you. In a split second they could do anything. I have two ponies. If something's pinching them, they could rear or buck. I don't let my friends ride, they're not allowed to for health & safety. YOU HAVE TO KEEP AN EYE ON YOUNG CHILDREN ALL THE TIME AROUND HORSES. We have tractors and teleporters, which lift heavy things. The teleporter is a big long thing. It has a cage to hold stuff. It's big and high, and someone wouldn't see you, so you have to keep out of the way. I don't think our tractor has a seatbelt. On the road Dad would wear the seatbelt but just on the farm, he wouldn't wear it.

Nicole Murphy, 4th Class, Co. Sligo

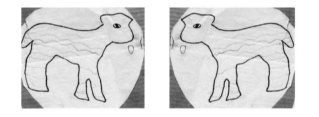

My granddad had a farm. I saw him **SPRAYING** with gloves and glasses on. When we used to go out playing, my Granddad said DON'T GO ON THE FARM TO PLAY, STAY AROUND THE HOUSE. He said don't go out because the gate is open. We used to be out playing by the cattle and he used to tell us to go up and play by granny's in case we got hit. I like the farm because you get to see all what's going on. If you go down on the farm you get to see something new every day.

Emma McManamon, 3rd Class, Co. Mayo

Some of the **CHEMICALS,** if you ate them, you could get a disease and you could die, or if you didn't wash your hands after touching them. I KEEP TELLING MY GRANDDAD TO WASH HIS HANDS. We've never had accidents with chemicals but I fell into a bog hole. I was walking through a waste ground and my granddad told me to go into that bit and it was a bog hole. I fell in, but I managed to get out. My granddad pulled me out, so he made up for it. It would be too dangerous to put the toys on the farm. There's a sign up and it says "This is not a playground. Always keep children guarded."

If you're milking the cows IT'S SAFER TO HAVE STEEL TOE BOOTS AND YOU NEED GLOVES MOST OF THE TIME, if you're feeding sheep or giving the calf an injection. You need goggles for some jobs. Like when you're using the chainsaw. ALWAYS HAVE THE EMERGENCY PTO STOP IN THE TRACTOR. If the key is stuck, you just break the glass and it stops.

Adam McMahon Coleman, 1st Class, Co. Sligo

I live beside the farm. There's only cows and sheep. I'm allowed on the farm but only with my dad. I pet the **LAMBS**. My brothers and sisters go on the farm sometimes too. My dad works on the farm. He tells us not to go near the bulls. You'd get kicked.

Hannah Rose Deane, Senior Infants, Co. Donegal

We're not allowed to go into the farm except when our football goes in. Then we have to ask our neighbour and she goes in and gets it. I saw a **SHEEP** in the field and she was upside down. There's something about if the sheep is upside down the gas can get to its heart, so I ran in and turned it the right way up. IF THERE WAS WATER OR OIL SPILT BESIDE THE SLURRY PIT YOU COULD SLIP AND FALL IN. If there was a dog or cat in the slurry pit, I'd leave it because if you tried to save it, you'd get killed. MY NEIGHBOUR GOT HIS LEG CAUGHT IN A MACHINE AND HE LOST HIS LEG. I was in the digger and I nearly fell out of it. I leant back on the handle of the door, and it popped out and my dad caught me.

Christopher Twydell, 5th Class, Co. Sligo

Our farm just has **PONIES** and a dog. I don't have anything dangerous on the farm, only when we're by this big lake where the ponies get their water, then we have to be very careful there. The ponies aren't too dangerous but you have to be careful not to let them go near anything flowery. Once I was wearing a flowery coat and they were trying to eat my arm! I like it most because we're allowed to stroke them as long as we're not wearing flowery coats.

Annabelle Frankham, Junior Infants, Co. Leitrim

My granddad has **PIGS** and a horse and the pigs make a lot of noise. The dog tries to get in the field. The dog is afraid of the horse and the horse is afraid of the dogs. If a dog was near the slurry or a cat, it could sink. I've been in the shed with the pigs. The pigs are very noisy and they are very smelly. And they're dirty. I'm not allowed in with the horse. Because it could kick you or charge.

Alice Curran, 1st Class, Co. Mayo

Chemicals. You have **BEESONS** and BVD and paracetamol and Pen & Strep - that's used if they have disease or something. You put it on the muscle. IF YOU DRINK THEM YOU'RE DEAD. If you have an old house, you can get a door on it, and put a lock on it and put a sign up. I'm the one who goes up and gets the chemicals. You have to be careful. Don't drop the bottles because they're glass and that's why we always have a lock for them and store them really high. My mum got a horse from a boy called Fred. I went into the garden with it and it just reared up.

I got to hold the horns when they were horning the bulls and I loved getting the blood all over me. IT IS A WEE BIT DANGEROUS DOING THE HORNING. THEY GO MENTAL. ONE OF THEM PULLED MY BROTHER AWAY AND IT DRAGGED HIM ONTO THE CRUSH. That's where the cows go down.

We had a calf that was born and it was just the size of a wee Jack Russell. The thing I like most is cutting silage and square baling. We have a 7-6-10 and we have a square baler and it drops it off and it's on a cage and whenever the cage is full, the door at the back opens up and the bale slides out and we have a quad and we lift the bales onto a trailer and we take it up to a silage trailer and then we take them up to the stack. And the sweat is pouring off you! We had all the McConnells down and all of us - all my brothers and sisters - that's why I like it and cutting the silage too, because everyone comes. It's safer then because if you do fall everyone will be there. And if you do fall off you land on bales.

Jason Arthur, 5th Class, Co. Donegal

NORTHEAST

How much does a **SILAGE BALE** weigh? It depends how you make it. If it's made in wet weather it could weigh a tonne, but a hay bale would weigh a lot less and a straw bale even less again. The best ones would be four foot by four foot. You get ones that are three foot and ones that are four foot.

We use the **QUAD** for fencing or drawing timber. We use it for places the tractor can't go. IF YOU'RE UNDER 16 YOU'RE NOT ALLOWED TO DRIVE IT. You can bring up to 22 tonnes of silage in a trailer. The pit can hold up to 1000 tonnes depending on what size it is. You get used to the smell of slurry.

The **SLURRY TANK** that goes on the tractor can hold up to 8,000 gallons. You just use that to draw slurry from one farm to another. The slurry pits are under the sheds and there are slats, which are made of rubber. WHEN YOU'RE TAKING THE SLURRY AND YOU'RE TAKING IT OUT OF THE TANKS IT COULD BE OPEN AND YOU COULD FALL IN IT. You use it in February or March. You put it on the grass to make it grow for the summer.

A **BULL** could be up to a tonne in weight. It depends how much they're fed. We've got five bulls. You put the bull out with the cows on the first of May.

THE BIGGEST TRACTORS HAVE 600 HORSEPOWER but they're not in Ireland. The biggest ones in Ireland are 400 horsepower. The best thing is there's something to do every day.

Patrick Smith, 6th Class, Co. Cavan

We just have **COWS** on our farm. We have 100 cows - all sucklers. They're about 5 foot high. THE PTO SHAFT IS DANGEROUS. IT SPINS AROUND. There's a thing on the tractor that you connect to it and there's a thing on the attachment and it's connected and the thing on the tractor spins around and the PTO shaft spins around. If it doesn't have its cover on and you touch it you can lose a body part. It wraps it around it and it comes off. MY LITTLE BROTHER'S TEACHER'S FATHER LOST HIS HAND BECAUSE OF A PTO SHAFT. The cover is plastic.

Fertiliser is dangerous because if you put it in your mouth you could burn your mouth. My dad told me. I was going to eat it one time when I was younger, but I didn't swallow it.

Donkeys like bread. One time I was beside a field and there were donkeys, and ducks and chickens. I went to feed bread to the ducks but the donkey got hold of it and he wouldn't let go. One time our bull's neck got so fat, he couldn't fit his head through the barrier to eat the silage, so we had to put the silage in the field with him.

Brady Maguire, 3rd Class, Co. Cavan

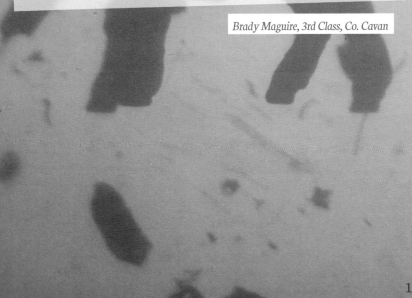

My neighbour was in the **TRACTOR** and he nearly drove into a wall. We're allowed to go everywhere but not in with the cows.

OUR JOBS ARE: TO CLEAN OUT THE SHEDS - CLEANING ALL THE POO OUT. I SCRAPE IT OUT WITH A FORK - NOT A FORK THAT YOU EAT WITH. I feed all the horses - with hay - and I bed them. You put soft hay in and they can sleep in it. We have seven or eight horses - and three foals.

Fionn Mullan, Senior Infants, Co. Meath

I was with one of my sisters and her **WELLY** got stuck in the cow poo and she was holding on to me and I said, let me go, or I'll fall in and she pushed me in and I fell face forward into the poo! At my granny's house, she has 3 ponies. When you're moving the cows, you need a stick to push them out of the way with.

The rollers are for flattening ground and stuff. THEY'RE QUITE BIG AND THEY'RE MADE OF STEEL. They can be different sizes. We've got a horse feeder - it's a big circle made of metal and you put the feed into it. But it always has poo on the outside of it. I've cleaned it a couple of times but it stinks.

Meadhbh Brennan, 4th Class, Co. Meath

Our farm has **COWS** and horses. If you stand behind a tractor and you didn't see another car coming it could reverse back and kill you. YOU HAVE TO STAND TO THE CORRECT SIDE THAT THE TRACTOR IS NOT ON. My dad and my granddad drive the tractor. Fionn kicked the ball in the field with the cows and he asked dad to go in and get it. Fionn cleans out the sheds – he cleans the horse poo and he gives them hay. I just go down to feed the horses. We're not allowed to feed the foals because they snap but we can feed the mammies because they don't snap.

Ava Mullan, Junior Infants, Co. Meath

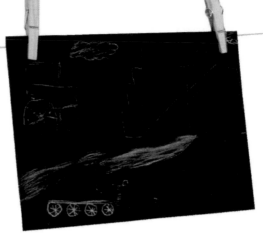

My dad has a **DAIRY FARM**. The best tractor wheels are Firestone or Goodyear. The tractor tyre could be 6 foot high. And the wee ones are around 4 foot. And the quad ones are 2 foot. The silage is cut around this time of year. You can get second cuts if the weather is good.

The pig slurry is stronger than cows. The slurry pit is always closed. You can slurry up until the end of October and after that you're not allowed because the ground's too wet. I help out with bringing the cows - we bring them in once and we bring them out once- to be milked. And I help with milking - washing the buckets and bringing the milk to the calves. Horning the cows: you have to get the thing with a hole on it and you plug it in to get hot. And you cut the hair so you know where the horn is and you have to tag the cow as soon as it's horned. And you have to fill in forms and there's a new thing where you have to send off their blood to the creamery. THEY DON'T ALWAYS WANT YOU TO SPREAD FERTILISER BECAUSE IT COULD GO INTO THE WATER. IT'S VERY POWERFUL STUFF. It makes the grass grow.

Conor McEnaney, 2nd Class, Co. Monaghan

I've been to Newgrange. It's a **PUBLIC FARM**. There was a lot of animals like hens, horses, cows and pigs and we went on a trailer and we sat in bales but it was all secure. We were not allowed to open the gates if it said. I liked looking at the animals and feeding them as well. I felt safe on the farm.

Abby Eogan, 4th Class, Co. Meath

We're allowed to play in the woods and in the **BACK YARD**. We had a tiny lamb called Brian but she was a girl. I help out sometimes getting sheep out and shearing them – I put them in the pen for Dad. We sheared them last week. It's confusing because there's so much going on. My brother separates the ewes and the lambs with a lever. He's only 7. The ewes go up a shoot to be sheared and the lambs go somewhere else. I have to get out of the way if Dad's driving the loader. He tells me just to be careful. I can tell when he's driving the loader because I can hear him and see him. It's like a really, really, really, really big forklift. It goes to one side. And the engine is at the back. There's only one seat in our tractor. We're only a bit taller than the wheels on the loader. ON THE QUAD YOU'RE SUPPOSED TO WEAR GOGGLES, A HELMET, BOOTS AND GLOVES – it says on the side of it. The silage bales are stacked on the far side of the sheep shed but we don't mess with them at all. I tried to push a hay bale once and I ran up against it, but I just fell over.

Emily Mangan, 4th Class, Co. Dublin

I've been on a farm on a school tour. There were **HENS**, and there was a goat and it bit me on the finger. And there was a horse and there were cows in the field. They said, don't go behind a cow and a horse because they can kick you. And they said DON'T OPEN UP THE GATES BECAUSE THE ANIMALS CAN GO AND HURT PEOPLE. And there were donkeys. We were allowed to feed the sheep with a bottle. There was a hole in the hedge and the sheep were getting out. And I saw a couple of scarecrows. And a dog to round up the sheep. Sometimes there's no gates on the barn and that's how the foxes get into the hens.

Gavin Nolan Hackett, 5th Class, Co. Meath

I've been to Sanmore farm. It was good because we were allowed to feed the **BULLS**. I saw ducks, donkeys. I got to see puppies and rabbits.

Amy Rhatigan, Senior Infants, Co. Monaghan

My granddad has a farm, it's only about 10 minutes from where I live. He only has **BOY COWS** because he doesn't want to be milking. My granddad says the combine is really big and THE DRIVER MIGHT NOT BE ABLE TO SEE IF THERE'S A CHILD THERE. You'd have to move very quickly, because if a combine got very close to you, it could be very fast sometimes. And it's very noisy. The combine is big.

It's only safe to play when there is someone in the field with us. My granddad needs the hay in the winter to feed the cows with. My granddad's slurry pit would be safe because he's got it all boarded up where the pipe goes through.

If the roller wasn't attached, you could probably push it. If you rolled it down a really steep hill you wouldn't be able to stop it.

Shauna Murphy, 2nd Class, Co. Meath

I am from **ROMANIA** originally and I've been living in Ireland for four years. When I was in Romania I went to the farm every weekend to my granny and granddad. They had sheep, cows, pigs and horses. Even here in Ireland, I go to the farm a lot. I like playing with animals. My dad's friend owns a farm. He has a little bit of everything. I'm afraid of the bulls. I went once to a farm and I saw a bull. I was on a trip with my friends.

Georgiana Ciornei, 4th Class, Co. Meath

My granddad has a farm. He has a **TRACTOR**. The wheels are huge. They're taller than me. The step up onto the tractor is quite high. They have a big shed for the bales. We tried to push a bale once and it took five of us to push it.

Emma Doyle, 4th Class, Co. Dublin

EAST

Wearing **WELLIES** is important so you don't step in cow poo or anything. Also if you had brand new shoes they might get ruined. I'm allowed to ride a pony. I rode on a horse in a festival. If you went in to give the cows the hay don't forget to close the gate again.

Ruby Nixon, Junior Infants, Co. Kildare

Keep safe with **HAY BALES**. Don't play on them. If they are stacked really high they could fall on you.

Lily Raben, 2nd Class, Co. Kildare

Stay away from **BULLS** because they could charge at you. They are so strong. A BULL IS REALLY, REALLY, REALLY HEAVY.

Their horns could stick into you. It would be sore. It would be really sore. You could die. You could fall on your back and break your spine. I'd like to know how strong a bull is. I think a bull could pull a car.

Toby McMorland, Senior Infants, Co. Kildare

My dad fell in a **SLURRY PIT** once but he got back out. My dad is from a farm originally. His friend got chased by a bull once. WE FOUND OUT THAT A BULL WEIGHS 192 STONE. I THINK IT'S ABOUT A HUNDRED TIMES HEAVIER THAN ME.

Hay bales are dangerous. My friend's horse nearly kicked her in the head, because the horse was very big and we were giving more food to the baby one. It's very mucky on the farm.

Faye Megarity, 2nd Class, Co. Wicklow

Do NOT GO NEAR MACHINERY BECAUSE IT COULD CUT YOUR HEAD OPEN. like combines and tractors and sprayers. The sprayer is a square with things sticking out. A person couldn't lift a bull. Only a giant could. THE HAY BALES CAN ROLL.

We have a stables. We still have a **HORSE** that we have to name. I'M NOT ALLOWED TO RIDE ON THE HORSES BECAUSE I'M ONLY FIVE AND A HALF. They're sort of dangerous. When you're behind them they're very dangerous but when you're in front of them they're not very dangerous. But they can bite. Don't go near the poison.

William Smith, Junior Infants, Co. Wicklow

Be CAREFUL AROUND THE SLURRY PITS. THE SMELL CAN LET OFF DEADLY GASES and if you fell in it would be hard enough to get out and you might drown. If you're on a farm and you want to go and see a dangerous animal make sure you go with someone who knows the animal. I really doubt I could outrun a bull. I think a bull could pull a tonne.

Most farms are in the **COUNTRYSIDE** and there won't be many cars around so it would be nice and quiet. I'D LIKE TO LIVE SOMEWHERE QUIET. YOU'D BE ABLE TO FOCUS ON THINGS BETTER BECAUSE THERE'D BE NO NOISE TO DISTRACT YOU. I live right beside the road. At night when you have to go to sleep there's a lot of cars going past. If you play football on the farm and the ball goes into a dangerous place, don't go after it. If there's an adult you might be able to get it back, but don't go after it.

Nathan White, 3rd Class, Co. Kildare

I went to a farm as part of a school tour. There were lots of animals and **TRACTORS**. The farmer was teaching us how to hold a lamb and how to know when the baby is ready to be born. The farmer told us to hold the lamb up by the front legs instead of cradled in our arms, because it's more comfortable for them.

THERE SHOULD BE SIGNS ON THE FARM TO TELL YOU WHAT TO DO. Like a sign for the chemical stuff. And a sign on the electric gate.

Milena Modesto, 6th Class, Co. Kildare

I was on a farm as part of a school tour. There was **CHICKS**, calves, lambs - all the baby animals. Don't go near hay bales. If you slide down them you could fall in. In our school we did an experiment to see how long it takes for an egg to hatch. It took 21 days. If it went over 27 days, you had to keep an eye on it. Our egg didn't have a chick in it. Don't go into the warehouse where they keep the poison and the fertiliser for the plants. THERE SHOULD BE SIGNS LIKE 'KEEP THE GATE SHUT'. Sometimes people say that the electric fence is on but it's actually off. But it puts people off.

Kerri McCann, 6th Class, Co. Dublin

We went on a farm for our school tour. There were **KITTENS** and sheep and pigs. I gave the sheep some milk and he pulled it back and I pulled it again and he pulled it back. My classmate was holding a chick and it peed on him! I think it would be fun to live on a farm because it would be very busy. The farmer is feeding all the animals. He has to wash them. DON'T LITTER ON FARMS. The wind might blow it onto the window of a tractor and the farmer wouldn't be able to see.

Erica Mae Bacani, 1st Class, Co. Dublin

My cousins live on a farm. It's near a freeway. They have a lot of animals and they also have a pet shop beside the farm. You can buy fish and hamsters and they have a lot of birds. They have **RAMS** and pigs and hogs and owls. They have a white one and a brown one and they have chinchillas, guinea pigs, mice and rats. They feed dead chickens to the owls.

Dean Harris, 5th Class, Co. Dublin

If there's **COWS** in the fields we try and stay away from there and we play around the field – not actually in it. Sometimes there are bulls in with them. One time my cousins did go in the field to make a movie and they were dressed in a cow costume. The other cows started running into groups. There's a farm right beside my school as well. There are always lots of tractors going by. We have to keep all of the gates closed. MY GREAT GRANDDAD FELL OFF A HAY BALE AND GOT THE HAY FORK STUCK INTO HIM.

Eleanor Stephens, 3rd Class, Co. Wicklow

The **BULL** is chasing the girl. She's wearing the colour red. The bull saw the red and ran. Now she's running away. If she fell the bull could trample her and she could die. THE BULL RUNS REALLY FAST AND HE'S VERY ANGRY. He has strong legs. The bull has come through the open gate. The girl opened the gate but she didn't see the bull. She was wearing a red pullover and she took it off and changed to purple when she saw the bull running towards her. The farmer should close the gate so the bull can't chase after people. ALWAYS CLOSE THE GATE.

Ciana Dunne, 4th Class, Co. Kildare

I live on a cow farm. We have over **320 COWS**. We have a horse and chickens and a pig as well. Pit silage is when the harvester puts it into the trailer and the trailer drives over to the farm and tips it and the loader pushes it all up. It can stack silage. It's like a tractor but it has no hitch. It only has a handler and a bucket. It's like a digger.

I'M NOT ALLOWED TO SPRAY SLURRY WITH MY DAD ON HIGH GROUND BECAUSE ONCE HE FLIPPED THE TRACTOR AND HE WAS IN-SIDE. The window was broken and he got out through the window. Summer is my favourite time of year because Daddy's at silage.

We do ploughing as well. The plough is like blades but they look round. Sometimes we do it around the end of summer. If the field is really bumpy we plough it in the summer - if there are lots of stones.

My dad's friend was looking at the PTO and he was going to take it off the back of the tractor and he stuck his hand in without looking. It was still on but he didn't know. It took his arm off and he fell into the slurry pit but his worker put him out.

Ethan O'Connell, 4th Class, Co. Limerick

SOUTHWEST

We have cows and **SHEEP** - a mix. It's good but bad in the same way living on a farm. It's dangerous and there's a smell. It's nice being out in the countryside. My favourite thing on the farm are the horses. I like feeding them. They're nice to be around. Spring is calving and summer you're making bales and in winter you put the animals in and feed them nuts as well as the hay you made over the summer. MY DAD WAS TRYING TO PUSH A BALE AND THE BALE ROLLED BACK AND HE BROKE TWO OF HIS RIBS. It might have weighed 20 stone, maybe a bit more. My dad was closing the gate to put a bull in and THE BULL KICKED THE GATE AND THE GATE CAME FLYING AND HIT HIM. A combine is like a big harvester. It's for corn. It's like a wheel thing in the front and it cuts the corn and then there's a shute at the back and it shoots it out into the trailer.

Kevin O'Connor, 6th Class, Co. Limerick

My granddad has a farm. He has **COWS** and sheep. They don't let us climb up on the bales and there's plenty of fences all around the fields and you can't go onto the farm without permission. My dad works in safety. When you spray water up, you have to be careful that it doesn't go on overhead wires otherwise you'd get electrocuted. Me and my friend found this thing about two people being killed on quad bikes that went out of control. One of them went into an ESB pole.

My friend's brother was shooing away the cattle and he saw a broken fence and he was trying to shoo back the animals and he wasn't looking where he was going and a post came down and it chopped off the top of his finger. And he was a good way back so he had to walk all the way home and it was bleeding.

Benjamin O'Dwyer, 6th Class, Co. Limerick

My farm is in north Kerry. We have a tractor and lots of machinery and cattle. We have fertiliser spreader, a slurry tank, a roller - it rolls the ground first and packs the stones deeper, because if there's any stones when you're doing silage, the harvester could pick it up and it could break the harvester. We have 3 tractors. One is International, but we don't really use that. One is Case International and the other one is New Holland. The New Holland is the best one because it's the newest and it's the easiest to drive. Most tractors don't have seatbelts, but I think you can buy them and install them yourself. I WOULD WEAR THE SEATBELT IF THERE WAS ONE.

I don't have any cows of my own, but I buy the calf and sell it. I go to the

MART and sell it. You go to the auctioneer and he'll sell it for you. And if the money's too low for the farmer, the farmer might tell him to go again and he might get more money for it. I also like the silage and the bales. The loading shovel is the thing that stacks the silage. But it doesn't have anything to do with the tractor. And it doesn't sink on the pit. It doesn't go down through the silage because it has thick wheels. PART OF WORKING ON THE FARM IS FIXING MACHINERY. I'll probably be a farmer when I grow up, because I like farming. Most of my friends are farmers as well. My brother's going to be 14 and he works on the farm as well.

Tadhg Griffin, 4th Class, Co. Kerry

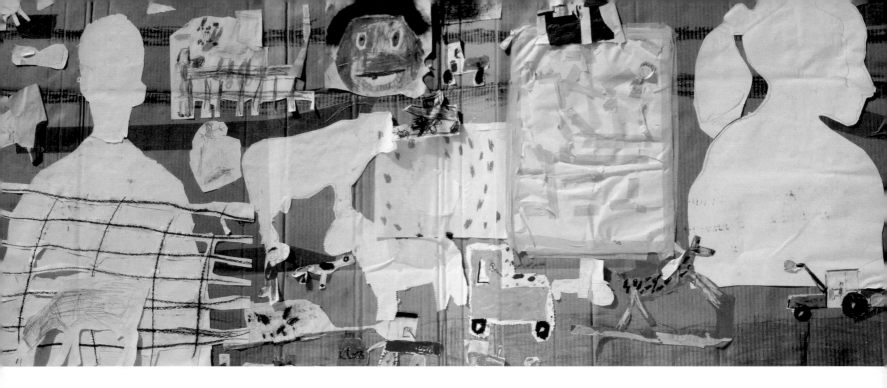

There's only **COWS** on our farm. Dad sold a few cows for me and Jack's Communion. We have about 20 cows. My dad does be baling fields and stuff and giving the cows food to eat and he has a job in Limerick as well. We'd be moving cows into the field and I have to stand in the road to make sure that they don't go down the road. And I help my dad to feed the cows. If we were putting stuff in the slurry pit I wouldn't go on the tractor.

In the summer you'd be baling and cutting silage. In the winter he has to put the cows in the shed. My two cousins have a quad but I don't go on it. YOU SHOULD WEAR A HELMET.

Cathal McElligot, 2nd Class, Co. Kerry

I live on a sheep farm – we have 1200 **SHEEP**. It's fun living on the farm. The best thing is silage in the summer because you get to draw the bales. We have a plough and a hay bob – it turns the hay. It has two wheels that turn around. The PTO connects onto it and makes it spin. It turns all the silage over and makes it into hay.

John Ryan, 2nd Class, Co. Tipperary

One of my nanny and granddads live on a farm with only **COWS**. I go there every weekday after school. In summertime I play with my little cousin Jane when she comes over. My dad owns a bull. I don't open the gates. It's mostly in Nanna and granddad's farm but I don't see it very much. FARMERS WORK HARD. IT'S A BUSY TIME WHEN CALVES ARE BORN. On Saint Patrick's night my dad had to go out because a calf was born. I LOVE THE FARM.

Eimear McCarthy, Senior Infants, Co. Cork

I live near a farm. My friend's dad fell into a **SLURRY PIT**. He was showing her some of the farm – bits she had never been to before and he fell into the pit, but they managed to get him out and he survived.

My friend's aunt got rolled over by a tractor but she survived. I don't know how she managed it.

Jessica Griffin, 5th Class, Co. Cork

I live next to a farm. We go down to see all the **LAMBS**. I'm not allowed to go in the fields, but I can ask if I want to. You should stay with whoever is working on the farm.

Lily Ashe, Senior Infants, Co. Kerry

I live on a farm and a campsite together. We have a lot of animals. We have 2 puppies, 2 dogs, 1 hen, 1 kitten, 2 cats, 1 cockerel, 3 hens, **2 DONKEYS**. We have composting showers and they're really warm. When horses are sleeping they stand up. We have three fields, but one field is full of horses. My dad is making hay at the moment.

Aisling Heapes, Senior Infants, Co. Clare

My godfather lives on a farm. We go there on a Sunday and we like doing all the farming and bringing the cows in and when we **MILK** the cows with my godfather, he would get the rations – they're like little green nuts except a bit softer. I really like farming. I would like to be a farmer.

Be careful of cows. And you have to be careful of tractors when they're moving and they could run over you. My dad's friend rides a quad. He goes really, really fast. HE DOESN'T WEAR A HELMET, because mostly he's on the mountains. The reason why the quad's wheels are so tough is because the ground is really stony.

Gráinne McCarthy, 2nd Class, Co. Cork

I live next to a farm. It's my uncle's. I like farming. He has nearly everything on his farm. I have to mind in case the cows stand on my toe. He has hens and **DUCKS.** He has a bull. It's usually in the shed. He has horns. My friend's dad has a quad and he fell off it and he broke his leg because the quad fell on him.

Corie Lynch, Senior Infants, Co. Limerick

I live on a farm. We have a **DAIRY HERD**. We have about 50 or 60 cows. On a dairy farm you have to milk cows but on a beef farm you don't. A silage wagon is kind of the same as a combine - it's kind of like a trailer but it has cogs in the front of it and it picks up the silage. If you got in front of it, it would draw you in. It's the same as the agitator, the cogs turn very fast. Don't stand in front of it and wave. You have to stand to the side of it.

An open slurry pit is dangerous. Sometimes there's not a scraper to scrape all the slurry down, there's a thing in the shed. I have an open slurry pit and a slatted one. The open one is kind of dangerous because there's no wire round it. My cousin was running and he didn't realise it was there. He fell and there was a bit of grass on it. Sometimes there's grass all over it. He was lucky.

My sister was looking for the calf and she fell into it as well. The gas comes off the slurry. When you're spreading the slurry and the tank is empty you have to let all the gas out, or else the tank can blow up and the tractor can go with it. You should close the window and the top window when you're letting the gas out because it can go all everywhere.

The best thing is testing cattle. You have to test them because badgers carry TB and they can pass it on to the cows. And if the cows have TB they can pass it on to a whole family. So you have to test the whole herd. They test them into the neck and the man goes away and he comes back 3 days later and if the lump is still there in the neck, then you know they've got TB. I kind of like those things and dosing them as well. My granddad has to open the cow's mouth and I have to squirt the stuff into them. If I come home from school and there's nobody else to do it, I do it with him.

Danny Fitzgerald, 2nd Class, Co. Cork

I live on a **COW FARM** – we have one hundred cows. On my farm we feed the cows and the donkeys and the lambs. We have a tractor on our farm and a digger. We have a hay bob and another tractor.

Samantha Streit, Senior Infants, Co. Cork

My uncle lives on a cow farm but I don't know how many cows he has. I go to my uncle's farm every Saturday. We usually have 7 UP and buns and then we go onto the farm and we go down to the barn where all the **CALVES** are and we play some games. Like 40/40 and hide and seek. Down there it's quite safe because all the tractors and cows are in the big machinery farm place. My uncle has two tractors and he has a loader on one of them and the other one's normal. The best bit is when we go down to feed the calves. Most of them come up really close to you and you get to rub them because they smell the nuts in the bucket.

Donal Reilly, 2nd Class, Co. Galway

We have a farm in County Cork. We have chickens and cattle and **MACHINERY** but we don't really use the machinery. Just for putting bales and all that. Our tractor is a Massey Ferguson. If there was a seatbelt, it would be like the car, you'd kind of get used to it. I like when the cattle start calving especially when my cow calves. I got her with my communion money. I've had her about two years. If the calf is a bull you definitely would sell it on but if it's a heifer you might keep it if it's nice.

I think I'll be a farmer. I don't bring my friends to the farm in winter because it's more dangerous. All the animals are in and around the farm. If you left a gate open and the cattle got out, you'd be in trouble straight away. Now is the best time, when all the animals are out. My dad works hard, because he's helping someone at the moment and he has to go to Kerry every day. My Mum does the chickens.

Pádraic O'Sullivan, 4th Class, Co. Cork

My uncle has a farm and my dad was raised on a farm. They have cattle and they do the planting as well. My cousin fell into the **SLURRY PIT** because they were at my uncle's barn and my aunt saw him and she managed to pull him out. He was very lucky that she saw him. If she hadn't seen him falling in, he would have died. You're not meant to wear loose clothes next to machinery like ploughs because it would pull your clothes and pull your whole body in.

Olivia Shortall, 6th Class, Co. Cork

My grandparents have a farm. It's a dairy farm. It has a **SLATTED UNIT**. One time my friend's granddad, he was taking the bull to the next field he had a rope around his thumb and the bull charged and his thumb came off.

Róisín Ní Riordáin, 4th Class, West Cork

SOUTHEAST

The girl in the **TRACTOR** is going into the pole and she hasn't noticed that she's running into the pole because she was putting on her lipstick. The other girl is saying stop! I've seen the front loader on my friend's farm. If the loader hit the wires, the girl in the tractor might get electrocuted. The front loader might knock down the other poles and wires.

Chafia Flynn, Senior Infants, Co. Wexford

We went to Secret Valley Farm for my friend's party. It has loads of animals. It has **SEALS** and goats. They have little toy tractors that you can ride on. And they have a big shaggy dog. You're not to climb on the bales. You can slip in between them.

Holly Hughes, 2nd Class, Co. Kilkenny

I went to the farm three times. I saw a cow, lambs, a **DEER**, goats, a pony, three pigs, geese, a duck, hens, hamsters, guinea pigs and I got to hold a chicken and a baby chicken. And I got to hold a tortoise. I saw a bull. He was happy. He wasn't even angry at me. The farmer let me ride on the bull. I was holding onto his horns. The farmer took me off. He was way taller than me. Taller than my horse. A bull might kick you if he's angry.

Mante Sladkeviciúte, Senior Infants, Co. Carlow

My cousins have a farm but we weren't allowed to play on it because it was dangerous. Some cows are **WILD** and they're dangerous. If you go near a bull when he's eating he gets very, very angry. My brother loves tractors and he's very small and he watches Bob the Builder and there's one of those on that. My uncle used to have a John Deere tractor but it wasn't working for him properly so he got a Claas.

Béibhinn Delaney, Senior Infants, Co. Waterford

My friend's farm was kind of an old farm. They had loads of **HORSES** in the stables. It was a horse farm. We just went around the stables. My friend showed us around.

Séan Hayes, 3rd Class, Co. Waterford

I have friends and I've been to their farms and their dads tell me what not to do. One of my friends she has **LAMBS** and chickens and her dad was showing us how to feed them and if you leave the gate open on the barn, they could all get out. My granddad had a friend and he said he was in a field with a bull and the bull ran into him and he got crushed against a gate and I think he got killed. We were playing on the hay bales and there were two stacked up on each other and my friend's foot got stuck and I had to pull her up. She got back up - it was okay.

Caoimhe Perdue, 6th Class, Co. Tipperary

THE PROCESS OF MAKING THE BALES IS DANGEROUS. If the **BALER** gets jammed by a stone or a clump of grass, most people put their hand in to unblock it. My uncle said that a lad in Cork he knew went down to unblock the harvester and put his hand in when it was left running and his arm came off. There's a handle on the side of the PTO and A LOOSE THREAD ON HIS JUMPER GOT CAUGHT ON THE PTO AND HE LOST HIS WHOLE ARM. AND HE STILL HASN'T GOT A GUARD ON THE PTO SHAFT! Sometimes in the machinery factory - that's where the mistakes are. Like say if the cog for an engine belt was put on wrong or loosely or something, then the belt is going round, it would slip off the cog and that could jam the whole thing.

A lad from Carlow - he's a contractor - he was putting on the belt onto the sprayer and he just tapped it over and he'd done it many a time before and just this one time his finger got caught between the belt and the cog and he was waiting for his finger to be cut off - he was shouting. There was a lad across the yard. He was shouting over at him. He couldn't be heard because of the revs of the tractor.

WHEN YOU'RE AGITATING THE SLURRY THERE SHOULD ALWAYS BE TWO PEOPLE THERE OR EVEN MORE. The dog fell in and the dog was sinking, he slipped, fell down into the slurry. The son came to help the father. The gas is what killed him. Then the other son came and the gas killed him. And the daughter came and he told her to stay away and she did and she survived.

Kieran Condren, 5th Class, Co. Wicklow

My friend was telling me that he fell out of a **TRACTOR**. He was getting out of the tractor and he just fell. There was only two steps on the tractor but it was high. I think he had to go to hospital. There could be rats in hay bales. There could be a lot of germs from the rats. If you found a dead animal, you shouldn't touch it because it might have germs on it. It might have gotten sick. Farmers are up early cutting silage. My friend Cormac, he's only starting silage on Monday. He's the fella that fell out of the tractor. He talks about baling and silage and harvesting. He makes it sound like it's hard work. But I think he likes living on a farm.

Oscar Brunnock, 1st Class, Co. Waterford

We're contractors – we do work for every kind of person. We have **DUNG SPREADERS**, loaders, we have every kind of machinery. We don't have a sower. The slurry is the most dangerous thing – spreading slurry is the worst or bales.

WHEN YOU'RE BALING A STONE COULD FLY UP AND INTO THE TRACTOR and could hit you on the back of the head and kill you. THE GAS OF THE SLURRY WOULD KILL YOU if you walk into the slatted house. BEFORE YOU AGITATE YOU HAVE TO GET OUT, OPEN UP ALL THE DOORS, AND AGITATE THE SLURRY. If you have butter and you want to make it all soft, like a mixer, it's like that.

When you're baling. If there was a big stone in the swarthe, the machine wouldn't see the stone, because it's all covered in silage. You'd hear a noise, it's like CLCLCLCLCLCLCLCL… And when you hear that noise you have to stop, turn everything off, get out and get away. You're supposed to leave it for 3-5 minutcs.

A little belt could be loose or could trip or grease could have got in the belt. If the belt slipped, the machine would cog up and if the belt is slipping around… If you put the belt back on, the PTO starts up again, and the stone could be coming along.

You're most likely to die with a PTO when you're using an agitator because there's a bar you have to turn to mix all the slurry because you're right next to the PTO. IF THE BAR WAS AWAY FROM THE PTO IT WOULD BE MUCH SAFER. You'd put your hand in to loosen the belt and the blade's going round. And SCHWUCK! it could take your hand off.

Spray in a coke bottle – sometimes you have to get the right amount. Say you need 500 mil, you could fill it up and someone else could come along and drink. Some sprays do look like coke, like spray for docks and rushes, that's the same as coke, it's blackish / brownish. It doesn't really have a smell but if you mix it with water it makes a horrible smell.

Jack Mullally, 4th Class, Co. Kilkenny

We have 4 horses and one foal, a **DONKEY** having a foal, three dogs. We had two pigs and nine chickens, but the dogs killed them. One of the chickens got run over by a lorry. I ride the horses. In the winter they're hard to look after, especially when there's no hay. You have to buy the haylage and the food. Most of our haylage – we had bales up but we had to sell it really cheap because the grass was so wet. I was feeding my pony a pear and the dog came up and tried to grab the pear and the pony got a fright and she nearly kicked him in the head. You have to think and not just do something. You have to think before you act. When you're riding you have to wear a helmet and I do be jumping sometimes. It's kind of dangerous. I fell off a few times and broke my wrist once. We had pigs but we ate them!

Niamh Ryan, 6th Class, Co. Tipperary

My granddad has a farm – a cow farm. And my childminder used to have a farm, which was a cow farm as well. My granddad has an **OLD TRACTOR** and there's no floor on it but it still works. He has loads of new kinds of tractors. John Deeres and stuff. They have proper doors and stuff. I'm not allowed on those ones.

My friend's daddy was taking the bales off the trailer and they fell on his legs and he broke his two legs. He had to go in a wheelchair. One of my uncles, he was playing on the bales with his sisters and the bales came down. Farmers get up really early and they go to bed really late. In the morning they have to milk the cows and in the evening they have to milk them again.

Tara McDonald, 2nd Class, Co. Wicklow

On some farms they kind of produce their own foods and things, like cheese and cream and butter and dairy and they'd have a vegetable garden as well and they'd have all their potatoes and they'd have an **ORCHARD** with pear and apple trees and they might have strawberries. And they'd sell their pigs and bulls and sell them on to factories. And they'd be killed and that's how we eat our ham.

That's how farmers make money. They sell products and they sell jam and things like that. My uncle has an orchard and vegetable garden. The orchard is always full of nettles. Usually you might have a well or a spring nearby. Lots of farmhouses are usually old because they're passed down through the same family. And you'd always have farm dogs.

There's a well in one of my uncle's fields. But they also have a thing, which collects rainwater, it's a big stone thing and it has a tap in it as well.

You're not the only one in danger. There's a tree that has this powdery stuff and it's not good for the animals - it can give them a reaction. You can't just leave the animals. And if a cow was in a field and you frightened it, and it ran around, it could affect their milk. You have to look after the animals. They could be in danger too.

Emma Ryan, 4th Class, Co. Carlow

We have a small farm and we raise **CALVES** on it. We have 14 calves. We got them off my cousin Jim. My farm is beside my granny's house. Granny runs the farm. We all help. I have two calves of my own. Lucy and Jimmy. I've had them since January / February time. We'll sell them when we want to. I won't be sad because I get more. We don't have cows that calve. We buy the calves and sell them on again when they're bigger.

We help granny feed them. I help her clean out the hay barn, and hunt them from field to field. It's not easy. Because they always go where you don't want them to go, they break out.

We ate our sheep! I appreciate what comes to my plate a lot more because I know the work that goes into it. When I'm older I want to be a vet.

Sophie Ryan, 6th Class, Co. Tipperary

THE STORY OF

"ONLY A GIANT CAN LIFT A BULL"

"In this book it features the dangers and how we can be safe on farms. 9,500 children entered a national competition and 86 were selected to take part in the making of this book." *Toby & Lily, Dublin West*

The project began with a national competition in which all schools were invited to submit stories, original artwork and safety messages from children all across the country. Over 9,500 children made an entry. From these entries, 86 children were selected as winners; their prize: to participate in a unique once-off workshop with Kids' Own Publishing Partnership in which, through a creative process with an artist and a writer, they would make their own book. In June 2013, Kids' Own artists Sharon Kelly and Orla Kenny, and writer Jo Holmwood, toured to six education centres across the country, where the workshops with the competition winners took place. The host education centres were: Athlone, Sligo, Navan, Dublin West, Tralee and Kilkenny. The children used collage, drawing and projection to create their artwork and developed their text for the book through conversations with the writer. Everyone worked together at the end of the workshop to create the page layouts that you see in this book. The winning entries that the children submitted can be seen here: http://www.flickr.com/photos/39766092@N07/sets/72157636936099814/

"Only a Giant Can Lift a Bull" is the result of all the children's work – a fantastic collection of their artwork, real-life stories, experiences, farm anecdotes, and of course, their safety messages. Here, all 86 children have a story to tell, which speaks to people all over Ireland about the crucial role that farms play in our society, but also about the need to be responsible for our children and families in these beautiful but dangerous work places.

"In gathering the written material for this book, I had lots of conversations with the children about their experiences of living on and visiting farms. Many children had stories to tell about incidents that had happened on farms. Others recalled happy memories of visiting farms or recounted tales they had heard from other family members. Ireland has a strong and proud farming tradition and the pastoral and bucolic nature of our nation is strongly reflected in the children's writing. In addition to their fond descriptions of their home pastures and farms, many children demonstrated very in-depth and technical knowledge about farm life, which reflects both the high level of responsibility that children have on farms as well as their exposure to many every day dangers."

Writer, Jo Holmwood

Scan the code with your mobile phone to see images of us making this book!

Health and Safety Authority · www.hsa.ie/education · Tel: 1890 289 389
For free in-classroom online courses check out www.hsalearning.ie

Kids' Own Publishing Partnership · Carrigeens · Ballinful · Sligo · Tel: +353 (0) 71 91 24 945 · E: info@kidsown.ie · http://kidsown.ie